Solving Cold Cases Vol. 2

True Crime Stories That Took Years to Crack

Andrew J. Clark

Disclaimer

All rights reserved. No part of this publication or the information in it may be quoted from or reproduced in any form by means such as printing, scanning, photocopying, or otherwise without prior written permission of the copyright holder.

Disclaimer and Terms of Use: Effort has been made to ensure that the information in this book is accurate and complete. However, the author and the publisher do not warrant the accuracy of the information, text, and graphics contained within the book due to the rapidly changing nature of science, research, known and unknown facts, and internet. The author and the publisher do not hold any responsibility for errors, omissions, or contrary interpretation of the subject matter herein. This book is presented solely for motivational and informational purposes only

Contents

Disclaimer..3

Contents 5

Introduction..1

The man who unleashed a 20 year bombing campaign against America 3

A vicious bomb attack while the whole world was watching 17

The anonymous corpse that came to be known as 'Tent Girl' 25

The mystery of the school girl who spent 10 years hidden in her boyfriend's home 33

The murdered boys whose killer was already in jail............39

A murdered man who was far from innocent 45

The killer who went on the run and battled against his extradition..51

Trying to track a man who was perpetually on the run 61

Arresting the man fifty years after his crimes.....................73

The case which came to be known by a licence plate 79

What happens when the rich and powerful protest their innocence in a murder case? 85

A butchered family who were killed together.....................97

Conclusion 105

Further Reading 107

Photography Credits 109

More Books from Andrew J. Clark 111

Introduction

Solving a criminal investigation is never as simple as it looks on television. With so many steps between the initial crime and the moment of conviction, the potential for a case to remain unsolved is always dangerously high. As well as those hard-to-solve minor crimes like petty theft, even the biggest and most complicated crimes have the possibility of becoming stuck at some point. So much of the process can depend on luck, that it should be no surprise to see that detectives and investigators often struggle arrive at that single eureka moment, that one instant of divine inspiration that might help them solve the crime.

In this book, we will be looking into some of the highest profile criminal investigations that have gone years without being solved. These are known as cold cases. When a case goes cold, the trail of clues runs dry and it becomes difficult to see an end point. But this book will examine those cold cases which have been solved. The murders, conspiracies, kidnappings, and other crimes contained within the book will be those which reach a satisfying conclusion. Even when everything looks bleak, either pure fortune or diligent work will be used to achieve a breakthrough.

We will travel the world to look over some of the most interesting and complicated cases which took years to solve. If you are at all interested in true crime, criminal investigations, or just examples of humans who never give up hope, then the stories contained within will be perfect for you. The true examples of cold cases in this book will cover despicable and deplorable crimes. Even when you might think the perpetrator got away, there will be one clue that finally got them convicted. So read on, and discover just how some of the world's coldest cases were finally solved.

The man who unleashed a 20 year bombing campaign against America

Suspect: Ted Kaczynski

Where: Across America
When: Between 1975 and 1995
Date of conviction: January 22, 1998

Even the highest profile cases are in danger of going cold. Over a twenty-year period, Ted Kaczynski's campaign of terror made him one of the most famous criminals in the United States. But no one knew his name. Instead, he masqueraded under the nickname, 'the Unabomber.' Despite the multitude of bombs he dispatched to locations around the country, police and investigators found it almost impossible to track him down. Despite the case being open for a number of decades, it would take a tip from a family member to finally close this cold case.

Ted Kaczynski was born on the 22nd of May, 1942. The eldest child in an Illinois family, he came close to dying as a young boy. An allergic reaction to medicine forced him to be placed into an isolated facility until he was able to recover. There have been numerous biographers who have suggested that it was this time in the facility that had a marked effect on the young Ted. The arrival of his younger brother David is also said to have been one of the pivotal moments in a childhood stranger than most.

Throughout his early life, however, Ted was known to be highly intelligent, and was a math prodigy. His academic successes marked him out as a genius. He was allowed to skip two grades during his first years in the school system, which contributed to him being considered different by the other children. Smaller, younger, but still much smarter, he was certainly unlike his classmates in some respects. He was involved in extra-curricular activities, notably the chess club and the German language group. At the age of just sixteen, Ted was admitted to Harvard University with a scholarship. He would study mathematics.

After graduating Harvard at a young age, Ted decided to continue his education. He moved to Michigan and both taught classes and worked on putting together his dissertation for the University of Michigan. This work would be met with rousing praise. He would stay at the university until he earned his doctorate. In 1967, now graduated, he moved out west to Berkley and the University of California to become a lecturer.

This was perhaps the first time he struggled. Ted Kaczynski found it hard to deliver his lectures, struggling to make eye contact. Soon after, he resigned from the position. This would be the first step towards Kaczynski's eventual move away from society. He resettled in Montana, using his time to build a small log cabin which was far removed from the rest of civilization. Here, he lived in isolation and spent his days reading, hunting for food, and refining his philosophy about the current state of the geopolitical world. Not a fan of the government, and not a fan of technology, these ideologies would lead him to begin a series of crimes that would terrify America.

In 1978, Ted tried one more time to reintegrate into society. He moved to Chicago and started to work in the same factory as his younger brother. He even began a romantic relationship with one of the supervisors at the factory. This soon took a turn for the worse, they broke up, and Ted consoled himself by writing crude poems about her. These limericks would get him fired. Worst of all, it would be his brother – another supervisor – who was tasked with dishing out the punishment.

Later that year, Ted assembled his first bomb. He made it himself at home, and sent it to a professor at Northwestern University. The parcel arrived and was opened by a security officer at the school. It exploded but only succeeded in causing minor injuries. By the time he moved back to Montana, he had already sent his second bomb to the same institution.

From his cabin, Ted began to devise a new list of targets. One of his chief focuses was American Airlines, with the company president receiving two bombs over the course of 1979 and 1980. After surmising that all of these attacks might be linked, the Postal Service, the FBI, and the Bureau of Alcohol, Tobacco and Firearms all worked together to set up an investigation. This would be known as UNABOM, an acronym which stood for **Un**iversity and **A**irline **Bomb**ing. Over the course of Ted Kaczynski's bombing campaign, he would become known as the Unabomber.

As Ted worked on his bombs, they became more powerful. Bombs sent to the University of California and the University of Vanderbilt both resulted in serious injuries for a professor and a secretary. The first death came in 1985, after a computer specialist was blown up by a bomb placed on the exterior of his shop. This would be the first of three people killed by the Unabomber, with over twenty-three people being wounded by the devices that he sent around the country.

The search for the Unabomber was one of the most extensive in American history. Part of the problem lay with Ted's genius intellect. Living alone in his cabin and working over the course of twenty years, Kaczynski found himself with the time and the ability to construct his devices without leaving any trace of his identity. The first clue the investigators had was a scrap of metal from one device, on which they thought the name Nathan might be inscribed. This would turn out to be incorrect. The second lead was a sketch of the suspect that police were able to have made after one of the devices was planted. This portrait was of a man wearing a hood pulled up over his head, large sunglasses, and a moustache. It was hardly enough to track down one man in a nation of hundreds of millions.

The FBI would construct several profiles of the Unabomber. They suggested that there was a consistent 'nature' theme to the bomber's work. This had to do with the small pieces of wood and bark Ted would place inside the bombs. This was a part of his strategy to leave behind fake clues in the bombs. These also included the imprinting of fake initials on the casings, all designed to lead the FBI down the wrong paths. At every turn, Ted Kaczynski was one step ahead of his pursuers. Over the course of twenty years, the authorities were never close to catching their target.

The breakthrough came when Kaczynski decided to let his political views become more widely known. During his time in the isolated Montana countryside, he had begun to construct a collection of his philosophical writings. Titled 'Industrial Society and Its Future,' it was a thirty-five thousand word long essay on the dangers of technology and capitalism. Kaczynski outlined his fears for the future of humanity and advocated a return to simple, rural living such as he enjoyed. The document was released and widely circulated among the press. Becoming known as the Unabomber's Manifesto, it was the first real insight into the political machinations behind the bombing campaign. This was published anonymously in September 1995. Even with the Manifesto, the FBI were no closer to their target.

However, there was one person who thought he knew the identity of the Unabomber. David Kaczynski had his suspicions about his brother's lifestyle and political views. He confessed as much to his wife, who encouraged him to go to the police. Before the Manifesto's publication, these suspicions seemed like a flight of fancy. After reading the Unabomber's words, however, David compared them to those of his brother. He searched through the archives of letters Ted had written to newspapers during the 1970s. They contained similar warnings about the dangers of technology, as well as many similar phrasings.

The FBI were still searching. Frequent press conferences asked for any information from the public. Up to this point, their suspicions pointed them towards someone in Salt Lake City who had spent time in San Francisco's Bay Area during the 1990s. This scant information, coupled with her husband's suspicions, prompted David's wife to encourage her husband to seriously consider whether Ted might be involved.

Following the publication of the Manifesto, the public response was massive — to the point of being overwhelming. A million-dollar reward led many to take a chance on providing information, and much of it was useless. Also, thousands of hoax writers began to send letters to the investigation headquarters. With the authorities tied up in this new wealth of information, David decided to take matters into his own hands. He hired Susan Swanson, a private investigator, to track down his now-estranged brother. Becoming increasingly convinced of his brother's secret identity, he hired a lawyer to ensure the evidence was presented in the right manner. Despite the brothers not having seen one another for a decade, David was still concerned for Ted's well-being. Having seen FBI raids in Waco and Ruby Ridge go horribly wrong, David wanted to ensure that nothing similar would happen to his brother. Knowing Ted's political leanings, he might not react well to a visit from the authorities and the situation could get very bad. This was exactly what David sought to avoid.

The lawyer hired by David was named Tony Bisceglie. Bisceglie in turn contacted a former FBI employee named Clinton Van Zandt. Van Zandt had been a hostage negotiator and had compiled numerous criminal profiles for the Bureau. Bisceglie requested to see the evidence that had been gathered together, including Ted's handwritten letters and the Manifesto. In the opinion of Van Zandt, there was a sixty percent likelihood that the bomber was Ted. By this time, the Manifesto had been released and widely circulated for six months. It was Van Zandt's recommendation that the lawyer and his client get in touch with the authorities.

In the early months of 1996, David Kaczynski's lawyer presented the FBI with an essay written by Ted in 1971. The investigators immediately recognised the similarities and compared the works. Linguistic specialists examined the writings and said they were almost certain to be from the same person. When aligned with the details of Ted's life and his political leanings, the FBI became increasingly sure they had their man.

Despite attempts to remain anonymous and to allow his lawyer to work on his behalf, the authorities quickly tracked down David Kaczynski. David and his wife were interviewed by agents and more of Ted's letters were handed over to the search teams. But David still sought to get assurances from the FBI that Ted would not be harmed. He even tried to ensure that his identity would not be known and that Ted would never find out. However, this information was leaked to the press over the coming months.

With the story in the possession of the media, and the search for Ted still not at an end, the director of the FBI requested that the television network CBS hold onto their information for one day longer. In April of 1996, the arrest warrant was drawn up and the authorities were compelled to act fast, before their suspect's identity was broadcast to the nation. A final attempt to gather more information resulted in the FBI searching through the records at Ted's former high school. Reporters were waiting for students at the end of the day and began to ask them what it felt like to share a school with the Unabomber. The story broke over the next few hours.

The warrant issued for Ted Kaczynski is not without its critics. Some have noted that there are paragraphs inside which suggest not everyone at the FBI was convinced that Ted was the Unabomber. There remained a split among the investigators as to his involvement. Despite the split, the media's involvement compelled the authorities to act fast.

Ted Kaczynski was arrested by the FBI on the 3rd of April, 1996. He was still living in the remote log cabin in the Montana countryside near Lincoln. He was dishevelled, unkempt, and unshaven. When searching through the cabin, the FBI agents discovered a range of materials used to make bombs as well as extensive journal notes detailing the Unabomber's various crimes and plans. There was even one bomb which had recently been completed and was set to be mailed to the next target. A draft copy of 'Industrial Society and Its Future' was found in Ted's possession, typed using his own typewriter. Finally, the FBI had reached the end of an almost twenty year investigation, one of the most rigorous in the country's history.

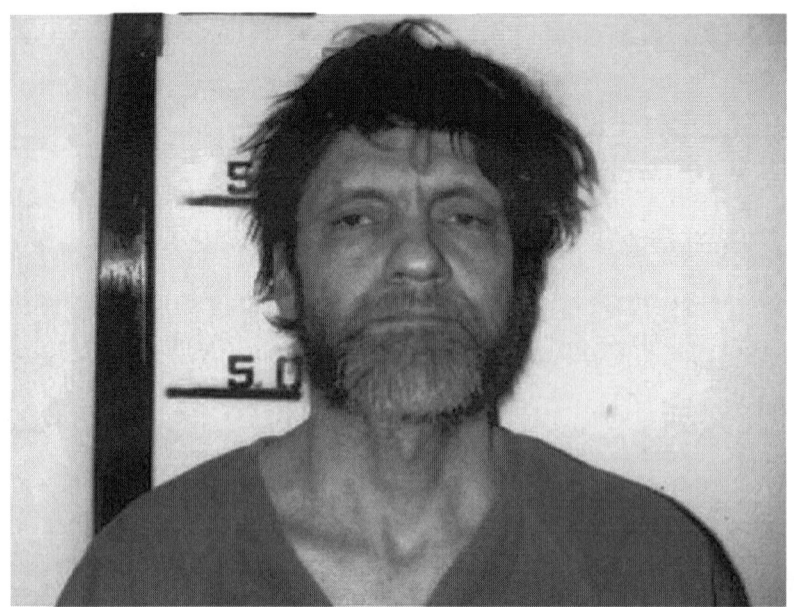
Kaczynski in 1996 when captured by the FBI

Worried about his brother being charged with the death penalty, David Kaczynski fought to keep his brother alive. Eventually, Ted plead guilty to all of the crimes in exchange for not being executed. He received eight life sentences which he is still serving to this day.

But the story does not end there. Some suggest that in addition to being the Unabomber, Ted Kaczynski may also be the Zodiac killer — another of America's famous cold cases.

The Zodiac Killer who terrorised the Bay Area in the sixties has never been identified and there was a concerted effort among some people to link Kaczynski to the crimes. Both crime waves were carried out by a highly intelligent person who had experience with and the capability to make bombs. Ted lived in San Francisco during this time, and the Zodiac Killer was also known to write to various newspapers with demands and threats of violence. While very few people would seriously suggest Ted Kaczynski was the Zodiac Killer, the involvement in two of America's most notorious cold cases (only one of which has been solved) is certainly an interesting footnote to the eventual capture and incarceration of the Unabomber.

A vicious bomb attack while the whole world was watching

Where: Centennial Olympic Park, Atlanta
When: July 27, 1996
Suspect: Eric Robert Rudolph
Date of conviction: August, 2005

Centennial Olympic park, 2011

Bomb attacks are some of the most difficult cases to solve. Once detonated, a large amount of the physical evidence is lost in the explosion, hindering forensic attempts to delve deeper into the crime scene. As we have seen with Ted Kaczynski, however, bomb attacks can usually be linked to a political motivation. While many terrorist groups choose to take the credit for the work, others simply vanish into the night and leave the authorities having to guess at the motivations for the attack. Because of this, bombing investigations can run a big risk of becoming cold cases. One of the most famous in American history is the bombing of the Centennial Olympic Park in 1996.

Atlanta, Georgia, was chosen as the host for the 1996 Olympics. As is typical in the run up to the games, a large amount of infrastructure building and development was carried out in the city. Millions and millions of dollars were spent improving the city's transport links and preparing for the influx of spectators which accompany every instance of the games. With the whole world likely to tune in via television broadcasts, it was vital that the city look and function at its absolute best. The Centennial Olympic Park was one of the key features of the designs. Intended to resemble a traditional town square, it was a focal point for audiences and spectators. As of July 27th, with the games in full swing, it was being used as a venue for a concert by the band Jack Mack and the Heart Attack.

The gig played into the night. While the crowds looked on after a long day of sports, Eric Rudolph began to plan his attack. He used a field pack from the US Military to hold together three pipe bombs that he had made at home. Around these pipe bombs, he fastened seven and a half centimetres of masonry nails. Not only would the bomb explode, but the nails would fly out and maim anyone nearby. He placed the field pack beneath a bench which was located near one of the large speaker stacks and exited the immediate vicinity. The device was fixed with a timer. Rudolph used an alarm clock strapped to dynamite and a number of containers. The steel plates he attached to the device would focus the blast.

Before the bomb could explode, someone noticed the strange package. As a directional device, Rudolph had carefully positioned the bag so that the spread of the explosion would cause maximum damage. After he had left, someone had shifted the position slightly. Even this tiny movement may have saved lives. Having spotted the strange bag beneath the bench, the authorities took action. They began to get people to leave the area and cancelled the concert immediately. The bomb squad were called. But before everyone could leave the area, and before the bomb squad could arrive, the device exploded.

One woman was killed by the bomb. Her name was Alice Hawthorne, and she was a middle aged woman from the nearby town of Albany. One of the nails strapped to the pipe bombs pierced deep into her skull and into her brain. Another death occurred when a Turkish cameramen intending to cover the Olympics ran towards the scene. En route, he was struck down by a fatal heart attack. Aside from these deaths, the explosion and the shrapnel wounded one hundred and eleven people.

The reaction was immediate. The then-President, Bill Clinton, made a national address which denounced the attack. He labelled it as an 'evil act of terror' and swore that he would use all of his power to track down the perpetrator. Despite the death, the injuries, and the destruction, the decision to continue with the rest of the games was nearly unanimous. All of the officials, athletes, and government authorities agreed that to cancel the games would be to surrender to the terrorist actions of the bomber.

The investigation began straight away. There was little evidence to be found and no one came forward to claim responsibility for the actions. Among those first detained were a pair of juveniles who were questioned by the police. Quickly found to be innocent, they were released without further charges. The first real suspect lined up by the investigators was a man named Richard Jewell. Jewell had been one of the first people to report the suspicious package to the authorities before the explosion. He had even helped to shepherd the members of the public out of the Centennial Park after the warning had been sounded. While he had initially been hailed as a hero, the following days began to see an increasing amount of scrutiny applied to his role in the bombing.

To the FBI, Jewell was an unknown quantity. With no one coming forward to claim responsibility for the attacks, the idea of a 'lone wolf' seemed to fit in with the reality of the situation. After speaking with a former employer, the FBI noted Richard Jewell as a 'person of interest' and his potential involvement was leaked to the media. Over the next days the authorities searched not only Jewell's home, but they began an extensive examination of his life and background.

Richard Jewell lived with his mother, and after his possible involvement was leaked to the press, he found it difficult to even go grocery shopping without being hassled and harried by the media. Later, he would confess that on many nights he was unable to sleep due to the noise coming from the media circus camped outside his home. After the investigation failed to find any evidence linking Richard Jewell to the bombing, he was exonerated of all suspicion. Once again, the media began to tout him as a hero. But this was not enough for Jewell. Having been hounded every hour of the day ever since he emerged as a suspect, he decided to file a number of lawsuits against the media. One of his requests was a formal apology. The case would rattle through the courts while the investigation struggled to find a replacement suspect.

After Jewell was exonerated, the FBI found themselves at loose ends. The case began to get colder. No new leads came until the early months of 1997. At this time, two new bombings took place in Atlanta. The targets were a lesbian nightclub and a clinic that provided abortions. The FBI were able to note a number of similarities in the manner in which the bombs were constructed. There were enough shared qualities for them to suspect the involvement of the same bomber. A further bomb attack – this time in Alabama – cemented the idea of a serial bomb maker. When examining the

Alabama attack, investigators were able to gather a number of clues, the most important of which was a partial read of a licence plate. For an investigation that had stalled, this was essential information.

Using the licence plate and a number of other clues, the FBI eventually found themselves arriving at the name Eric Robert Rudolph. When named as a suspect, Rudolph took to the road. At the time, the FBI believed that he had intentionally vanished into the Appalachian Mountains, difficult terrain where he would be hard to track. Rudolph knew the area from his childhood. To try and track him down, the FBI included the suspect on their '10 Most Wanted' list and even posted a reward of $1,000,000 for any information that might lead to his capture. It would be October of 1998 – more than two years after the first bombing – that the authorities would officially label Rudolph as the number one suspect in all four attacks.

Eric Rudolph spent five years running from the police. He was finally caught in 2005, when a rookie officer arrested a burglar during the break-in of a Save-A-Lot store in the early hours of the morning. A short time later, Rudolph plead guilty to all charges, including the bombing of Centennial Olympic Park. His reasons for the attacks were attributed to his religious and political views. Rudolph released a statement in which he said the 1996 Atlanta Olympics was an event generating global attention. Recognising the huge amount of effort and money the government had spent organising and securing the games, he sought to embarrass the regime for their legalisation of abortion. His end goal was to cause the games to be canceled, or at least to destabilize them enough as to cause major financial harm to those who had invested. His attacks on the lesbian bar and the abortion clinics were similarly motivated. He received a life sentence for the Olympic bombing, as well as three terms of life imprisonment for his other attacks.

Since then, Rudolph has officially apologized for the injuries and deaths he caused. He was, he says, angry at the government rather than individuals. He has also written a book of memoirs, the royalty check for which was seized by the government in order to go some way to paying back the damages he had caused. After their initial investigation, it took the authorities two years to finally recognise Eric Rudolph as their suspect. It took longer still to catch him.

The anonymous corpse that came to be known as 'Tent Girl'

Victim: Barbara Ann Taylor

Where: Georgetown, Kentucky
When: May 17, 1968
Suspect: unknown
Date of conviction: N/A

Not every cold case is completely solved. After many years of chasing down loose ends and trying to find out any information about the most mysterious crimes, any kind of breakthrough can be regarded as progress. The most distressing and disturbing crimes are often those where we have no information about the people involved, and are forced to leave them in limbo while we try to gather information about who they are, how they died, and who exactly is responsible for their fate. When just one of these questions is answered it can feel like a huge relief, especially when it had been looking like the case may never be solved. The story of Barbara Ann Taylor, otherwise known as 'Tent Girl,' is one such example of this kind of cold case.

The story of the Tent Girl begins in mysterious circumstances. A man named Wilbur Riddle was working alongside Route 25, scavenging for any kind of glass insulators that he might be able to recover. While he was searching, he happened to come across a pile of bound green material. Taking a closer look at the canvas tarpaulin – the material that is often used to manufacture tents – he noticed that there appeared to be a body inside. It had been there for some time and was already badly decomposing.

Riddle alerted the police. The investigators arrived and took away the canvas with the body inside. Back at the police station they performed an autopsy, but the extent of the decomposition meant that they were unable to identify the body. Without the ability to even put a name to the corpse, the police were unable to make any kind of list of who the suspects might be. They were at a dead end. They had a body, but had no idea who it was, how it had arrived at the road side, or who else might have been involved in the death.

Resigned to a lack of information, the authorities undertook it upon themselves to bury the woman. They took her to a cemetery in Georgetown, and buried her under a headstone with the name by which many had come to know her: Tent Girl. The headstone had been donated by a local person who had felt sorry for the girl, with the stone having an inscription to notify people about the circumstances of the burial. There was an engraved picture bearing the only likeness available, put together by the police sketch artist. There were the bare details of the case, telling how she had been found on the 17th of May, 1968, as well as the location where she had been found, a possible date of her death, and an estimate of her age. Police has guessed that Tent Girl had been no older than 19. Information such as her height, weight, and the colour of her hair were also written on the stone. Should anyone ever be seeking out a missing person, the police hoped that the details on the headstone would provide them with any answers they might require.

With little else that they could do, the police closed the case. Nobody came forward claiming to have known the girl, there were no guesses as to who she might have been, and nothing that even resembled a clue in the investigation. After the burial, the unidentified body became part of the local folklore. It became a ghost story retold among teenagers and occasionally people would visit the gravesite to learn more about the strange case of the murdered girl.

It would be thirty years before we even came close to knowing what happened. While the police had been unable to find any leads and had since moved on to other cases, one man had not given up.

In 1998, Todd Matthews finally managed to piece together the puzzle. Todd was the son-in-law of the man who had originally found Tent Girl, Wilbur Riddle. The case had fascinated him for a long time and he had made it his personal mission to find out more about the missing girl. After decades of searching, he came across a missing persons report for one Barbara Ann Hackmann Taylor.

Todd Matthews had spent a huge amount of time going over every single missing person's report that was filed shortly before and after the body was discovered. By collecting together all of the available information about the missing people and about the body, he was able to find correlations between certain cases and the corpse his father-in-law had found by the round. While he had gone down a number of incorrect routes, he eventually came across the name of Barbara Ann Taylor in the late nineties.

Barbara Ann Hackmann Taylor, known as 'Bobbie' to her friends, was born on the 12th of December, 1943. She had been reported missing from her home in Lexington, Kentucky (a place just fifteen miles away from the Georgetown road where the body was found.) Her information had been recorded and filed away, but no one had matched up the story of this missing girl and the unidentified Tent Girl. Once the records were digitized, it became possible for Todd Matthews to broaden his search using the internet. He took the information that he found, as well as details about Tent Girl, and passed them along to the Hackmann family and what was left of Barbara's estate.

Todd contacted the family with the suggestion that the person known as Tent Girl might be their daughter. They agreed to take part in a DNA test and the body was exhumed from under the donated gravestone. Once the test came back, the story was confirmed — Tent Girl was Barbara Taylor. Rather than move the body, the family instead chose to leave Barbara where she lay. They added a second stone detailing the deceased's true identity and telling people of what had happened. They added a presumed date of death, as well as well wishes from the surviving family members who finally knew where their little girl had gone.

Though Tent Girl has now been identified, the police have still not discovered any fresh leads into who might have killed her. There have been suggestions that Barbara's husband, George Earl Taylor, might have been the one who committed the murder and disposed of the body. But no evidence has ever been found. George Taylor died in 1987 after battling cancer. With his death, we might have lost any chance of knowing exactly what happened to the girl wrapped in the canvas tarpaulin and dumped by the road.

One interesting footnote to the story is the future endeavours of Todd Matthews. After helping to identify Tent Girl, he went on to establish a group known as the Doe Network. The group runs a website which helps collect together the information needed to pair missing person's reports with the decedents of the possible victims. After his work on this case, he hoped to be able to solve similar cases in the future.

The mystery of the school girl who spent 10 years hidden in her boyfriend's home

Victim: Tanya Nicole Kach

Where: Pennsylvania
When: February, 1996
Suspect: Thomas Hose
Date of conviction: 2006

Not every cold case is a murder. Sometimes, the missing person is alive. However, because of the pain and the amount of time that has passed, people have to come to terms with their loss, and they assume the victim has died. If the person reappears, there is a period of joy, shock, and adjustment, and a deep emotional confusion for both the victim and the victim's family. In such situations, it can be difficult for the victim to reintegrate into society. Sometimes, after years of being presumed dead, the victim reappears. Sometimes they can tell us what happened, they and their family can work together toward a normal future. Other times, they facts of the matter are not quite clear. The case of Tanya Kach is one such incident.

Tanya Nicole Kach was born on the 14th of October in 1981. She is most famous for the period of ten years when she was forcibly held against her will by Thomas Hose. Hose was much older than Tanya, and worked as a guard at the school where she was a student. The two had become friends and it was not uncommon for them to be seen talking between classes or when passing one another in the corridor. Eventually, Tanya began to avoid her classes in order to spend more time with Hose. During one of these spells of truancy, the pair kissed for the first time. After courting for a short while – all in secret – Hose convinced Tanya to leave her family and to come and live with him. She agreed and left home in February of 1996.

But it was not the romantic relationship she had pictured. For the next four years, Tanya was not permitted to leave the home. Thomas Hose shared a home with his son and his parents, and had to go to extreme lengths to hide the fact that Tanya was living in the house. She was only permitted to live on the second floor of the home, consigned to a particular bedroom. Instead of a toilet, there was only a bucket. By the time the year 2000 came around, Hose had strived to invent an entirely new identity for his hidden prisoner. Her new name was Nikki Allen. After this identity had been constructed, Hose felt it was allowable for 'Nikki' to meet his parents, and to inform them that she was be moving into the house. She was even allowed to leave the home after this, but was forced to return before a certain time. It would be six years before she was able to escape.

During this time, Tanya was listed as a missing person. As in many cases of missing people, trying to track her whereabouts was tough. Not sure whether she had been captured or left of her own free will, the police were hampered in their search. The fact she had departed under her own volition meant that few clues had been left behind. The case went cold.

After Tanya was allowed to leave the home, she met a man named Joe Sparico, a greengrocer, who she got to know. Eventually, she revealed her real identity to him and told him about her situation. He agreed to help her escape. The shopkeeper informed the police and, soon enough, they descended upon Hose's home to free the captive young girl.

In the following weeks, Tanya seemed happy to be reunited with her family. In the years since, however, she had become gradually estranged. She has since become engaged and has become part of a family, and is now the step-mother to her betrothed's little girl and boy.

But the story does not end so simply. Thomas Hose has challenged Tanya's version of events. Backing him up are his family and the shopkeepers from around the area where she was supposedly imprisoned. When Tanya first left her family, Hose was madly in love with her. That feeling of love persisted throughout the years they spent together. According to him, it was Tanya's idea that they secretly move in to the same home. During this time, she divulged personal information, such as the fact that her step-mother had abused her. This has been denied by her family. Similarly, Tanya's reputation had been that of a 'troubled' young girl. She had previously been included in four separate police reports and stories of her playing truant and running away from home were not uncommon. As such, she does have some problems with credibility. It was Hose's allegation that Tanya wished to move in with him because she felt unsafe in her current home. There had even been suggestions that Tanya would become his 'ward-of-state,' with her care set to legally transfer from Tanya's parents to Hose. Added to this, Tanya's reputation as a compulsive liar and as a violently uncontrollable teen led her to experience difficulties in her home life.

According to Hose, it was never the plan that Tanya would remain hidden in the family home. They had planned to change the colour of her hair and allow her to leave the premises. He suggests that his parents had known about her for years and frequently referred to her as being his girlfriend. This is a story backed up by Hose's parents, who even said that she helped with the cooking of dinner on a number of occasions. Even when masquerading under the name Nikki, she referred to herself as Tom's girlfriend.

Thomas Hose was charged with – and plead guilty to – charges accusing him of statutory rape in 2011. Because Tanya was a minor at the time she went missing, Hose was prosecuted within the law. Despite the statutory rape charges, there were no charges of kidnapping.

Ever since she has supposedly escaped from captivity, Tanya has made numerous attempts to sue a variety of government organizations, such as her local school and the police. It is her accusation that they failed to protect her. Every single one has been thrown out of court.

From a cold case, to a solved cold case, to a controversial incident, there is very little that we know for sure. We do know that Tanya wrote a book about her events, but critics have found it hard to take at face value. Despite being a cold case almost ten years unsolved, it feels as though there is still more to come in the case of Tanya Nicole Kach.

The murdered boys whose killer was already in jail

Victims: Charlie Keever and Jonathan Sellers

Where: San Diego County, California
When: March, 1993
Suspect: Scott Erskine
Date of conviction: September, 2004

Please note, this chapter contains a graphic description of a crime.

One tricky problem faced by those investigating cold cases is the absence of a suspect. When gathering together evidence and positing theories, the ability to follow and investigate a person under suspicion can often lead to the clue that blows the case wide open. However, when there is no suspect, this is impossible. In some circumstances, the suspect has fled the country. Sometimes they might have died. Other times, they have been arrested for other reasons. In the case of the murders of Charlie Keever and Jonathan Sellers, the investigation was slowed down by the authorities' inability to find a man they already had in custody.

The murder itself occurred on the 27th of March, 1993. At this time, Charles Allen Keever was thirteen years old. He had been born in 1979 to Lisa and Michael and was the youngest of the family's three children. After the crime emerged and the case stalled, his grandparents would die before they discovered the identity of Charlie's killer. Jonathan Sellers was four years younger. Born in 1983, he was aged just nine years old when the killer struck. He was a middle child, the fourth of six and just a couple of minutes younger than his twin sister.

On the 27th of March, Charlie and one of his brothers decided that they would spend their Saturday riding bikes. Before they could leave, a last moment rearrangement led to the brother staying behind and Jonathan going with Charlie. Jonathan's twin sister Jennifer asked if she could join them. The boys had no inclination to let a girl come and play with them and Milena Sellers, Jennifer and Jonathan's mother, told her to let the boys leave without her. Instead, Jennifer stayed at home that day while their boys went to ride their bikes.

At around twelve o'clock in the afternoon, the two boys left and took their bicycles to a nearby fast food restaurant named Rally's. Rally's was part of the Palm City neighbourhood in San Diego, and was one of the boy's favourite places. Following their visit to the restaurant, the boys took their bikes and made the short journey to a local pet store. Here, they took a little time to play with the cats and the dogs that were on display. They even had a chat with several people in the store, including the manager and a number of other customers. These people would be the last to see either of the boys alive, ever again.

According to the reports issued by the police, it seems as though the boys took their bikes and rode a short distance. Whether they did this under their own volition or whether they were lured by another person is not known. Their destination was a temporary, igloo-styled fort that had been constructed from the brush found along the Otay River. This would be the spot where Charlie Keever and Jonanthan Sellers were molested and then killed.

Their bodies were not found until the following Monday. On the 29th of March, a man riding his bike a couple of metres from the undergrowth, and happened to see the bodies of Charlie and Jonathan. The authorities were called, and they began a sweep of the area. When they were discovered, Charlie Keever's head was on top of a pile of clothing belonging to both boys. When examining the bodies, the police found that Charlie's genitals were not only bloody, but they were covered in bite marks. As would later be concluded by the autopsy report, these marks were inflicted when the boy was still alive. When looking even closer, the police were able to take DNA samples from the presumed killer from the dead boy's mouth. Jonathan was elsewhere. The killer had taken him a short distance away and hanged him from one of the area's castor bean tree using a length of rope. Jonathan's legs and arms had been tied up and a gag had been placed into his mouth. His lower half was naked. The investigators noted how tightly the rope had been wrapped around the boy's neck and that his genitals has also been desecrated.

Despite the presence of the DNA sample, the police found it incredibly hard to nominate a suspect. While the boys had been seen alive in the pet store, there was no one who had appeared to approach them and no one who could be described as having lured them to the riverside. The investigation continued for a long time, but there were few witnesses and few leads.

As the process of trying to catch the killer of Charlie and Jonathan slowed down, the family were not prepared to let the criminal escape. Most concerned was the mother of Charlie Keever, Maria. Maria Keever took it upon herself to catch the killer and chose to become a private detective in order to make up for the flagging police interest. She got a hand gun, and decided to go undercover amongst the local homeless community. After spending some time in disguise, she decided that she had a suspect. Taking her information to the police, she demanded that they investigate the person she felt had been responsible for the murder of the two little boys. The authorities took Maria up on her offer and looked into the suspect. Despite Maria's insistence, they found no information linking the suspect to the crimes and exonerated the suspect of all suspicion.

The real clue to the capture would arrive in 2001. The evolving DNA database threw up a lead — a man named Scott Erskine. The DNA taken from Erskine provided a match against the sample taken from Charlie Keever. At the time of the match, Erskine was already in jail for a rape he had committed in the months following the murder.

Erskrine mug shot

The case took two years to come to trial. Scott Erskine was charged with two murders, as well as the additional counts such as oral copulation, sodomy, and torture. After a short trial, he was found guilty. Following much deliberation on behalf of the jurors and the judges during the sentencing phase of the trial, the Californian court gave Erskine the death penalty. He has been sent to San Quentin State Prison where, as of the time of writing, he currently sits on death row.

A murdered man who was far from innocent

Victim: Andrew Kissel

Where: Greenwich, Connecticut
When: April, 2006
Suspect: Carlos Trujillo
Date of conviction: March, 2008

Very often, criminal investigations can overlap. One person's involvement in one case does not preclude them from being involved in another. Likewise, one person being the victim in on instance does not necessarily meant that they are free from guilt in another, or vice versa. The murder of Andrew Kissel in 2003 involved a set of circumstances such as these. After having been accused of large scale fraud, Kissel was murdered, and it was a crime that took many years to solve. As the potentially guilty party in one case, he was the victim in another.

Andrew Kissel was a real estate developer in America. He was fifty years old by the time he faced his first series of serious allegations. During the years 1995 through

2002, it was suggest that Kissel had abused his position on the board of a co-op group where he was the treasurer. The properties were located at Manhattan's 200 East 74th Street. His position involved a great deal of trust, and his partners and associates granted him a large amount of autonomy and exclusive control of the group's bank account.

Kissel took advantage of this position and began to arrange for a refinancing plan to be implemented, which would allow for the creation of a reserve fund intended to finance the building's upcoming renovations. While this had been the original plan and was agreed upon by the group, Kissel was accused of siphoning funds away from the project and into his own personal accounts. Using a series of forged signatures and clandestine arrangements, he embezzled an amount to the tune of almost $4 million. But he was caught. Fellow members of the board managed to figure out the plot and confronted their treasurer. Pleading for mercy, Kissel offered to pay the group back $4.7 million if they withheld the information from the public. Should it emerge that he had stolen the money, it would ruin his reputation.

The group agreed. They entered into a civil settlement with Andrew Kissel and were prepared to accept his payment. This pleased Kissel. Relieved, he thought that the matter had been settled and that he had escaped the possibility of the matter going public. But it was not to be. A Manhattan grand jury found cause to charge Andrew Kissel with grand larceny, among other crimes, because of the huge amount of money he had embezzled and then agreed to pay back to the board. After abusing his position as a treasurer, Kissel was facing a huge law suit and the threat of having to pay back all of the money right away.

The problem facing Kissel was where the courts would take their money. As a collector of expensive possessions, he had gathered a number of very costly items that he would rather not have to give up. Among his most treasured possessions was an eighty foot Lazzara yacht, something which had been valued at almost $3 million. There was also the question of his classic cars. One of these, a Mercedes from 1957, was valued at over $400,000.

Another of these was one of the famous cars from the TV series 'Knightrider.' A 1984 Pontiac Trans Am, it had been used in a number of episodes of the cult classic. Eventually, this car would be listed on eBay. Proving to be a popular choice, the bidding opened at twenty thousand dollars. After questions were raised about the authenticity of the vehicle, the item was pulled from the site. After this authenticity was obtained, the car was relisted, again starting at $20,000. It eventually sold to a man who was a friend of the original creator. With a need to pay back close to thirty million in bad debts, Kissel was right to be worried that the authorities would come for his prized possessions.

But that would soon pale in comparison to the troubles he was about to encounter. In 2006, realising that things were taking a turn for the worse in terms of his growing debts, the Kissel family were forced to move home. Having failed to pay the rent in almost six months, Andrew Kissel owed his landlord almost fifteen thousand dollars. After talking to the landlord, they agreed to leave the property. When the members of the removal service arrived at the home to help with the family move, they discovered that Andrew Kissel had been murdered. He was found with his limbs bound, hidden away in the basement. He had suffered from a series of stabbings, and died there in the home.

The case was both a media sensation and a difficult one to solve. Due to Andrew Kissel's history of fraud and embezzlement, the media were not on his side from the start. Since he had already been found guilty of one crime, some even went as far as to suggest that this was Kissel's comeuppance. Some suspected the fellow members of the co-op board, while others suggested that his wife might even be involved. All would be investigated but none would be found guilty. The case went cold.

It was two years before the real murderer was found. Carlos Trujillo was Andrew Kissel's chauffeur. He and his cousin Leonard became suspects in the death. The pair were arrested in 2008, after the authorities had discovered a credit card belonging to Kissel inside Carlos's home. They linked the stolen credit card to the murder and, during the interviews of the two cousins, they uncovered a murder conspiracy.

During the trail, the prosecution asserted that the reason for the murder was the worry that the Trujillo cousins might be exposed by their criminal boss. They had both helped Andrew Kissel to launder the money he had embezzled and were concerned – after Andrew Kissel had been caught – that they too would be facing prosecution. While the prosecution team suggested this as a motive, the jury were not so convinced. Carlos was charged with both murder and attempted murder. While he plead guilty to the latter, he remained insistent that he was innocent of the former. Leonard was charged with conspiracy to commit murder and with manslaughter. He plead guilty to both, going so far as to offer testimony against his cousin. Carlos received a sentence of six years in prison while Leonard received a sentence of twenty years. Despite Andrew Kissel's worry that the authorities would strip him of his favoured possessions, it was his partners in crime who would rob him of the most important possession of all.

The killer who went on the run and battled against his extradition

Who: Holly Maddux

Where: Philadelphia
When: September, 1977
Suspect: Ira Einhorn
Date of conviction: October, 2002

One of the most common difficulties in closing a cold case can be catching up with the criminal. Should a suspect go on the run, then being able to track them down conviction them can be very difficult. This is made even harder when the suspect crosses an international border. Depending on the country to which they flee, being able to apprehend the suspect can become a bureaucratic and diplomatic nightmare. Even more difficult can be trying to track the person in a foreign country, especially if they do not want to be found. This was the case in the murder of Holly Maddux. When her murderer – dubbed the unicorn killer – fled the country, it took a huge amount of time to track down the man responsible for the homicide.

The man was Ira Einhorn. He was a well-educated person, having attended the University of Philadelphia. After a middle class upbringing, he began to get increasingly involved in counter-culture movements during his academic career. He had a special interest in environmental groups, as well as anti-war and anti-establishment collectives. During the 1960s and 1970s, when he was a young man, involvement in these kinds of groups was not unknown. He even earned himself a nickname, 'the unicorn,' based on the fact that his name when translated from German meant 'one horn,' the German word for a unicorn. One of the biggest events in which he was involved was Earth Day in 1970, though fellow organizers have sought to downplay Einhorn's involvement ever since.

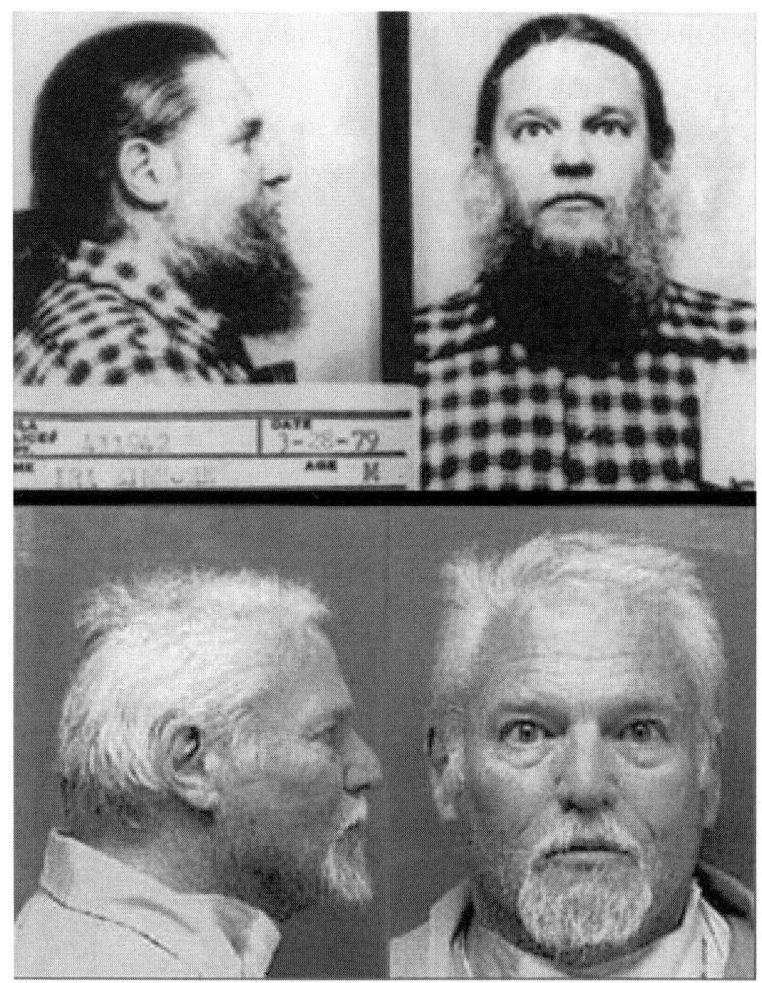

Top: Einhorn mugshot in 1979 – Bottom: 2001 mug shot in the U.S.

Ira Einhorn and Holly Maddux were in a relationship for five years. Herself a graduate of Bryn Mawr College, the Texan girl reached the decision to leave Einhorn in 1977. At this point, she was in the process of moving to New York and had already begun a separate relationship with a man named Saul Lapidus. After breaking up with Einhorn, she returned to their apartment to collect a number of her possessions. She would never again be seen alive by any of her friends or family members.

Her disappearance was soon noticed and reported to the police. When following up on these investigations, the local police force questioned Einhorn. He claimed that she had left the home to go and buy some tofu, but he never heard from her again. With little evidence to follow up on these answers, the police marked her down as a missing person.

Weeks later, neighbours would begin to complain about the smell coming from the flat where Holly and Ira used to live. The authorities were called, and in light of the circumstances, they became suspicious about the smell. It would take eighteen months for the body to be found. Despite the frequent complaints and the lack of contact from Holly, her body was not discovered until March of 1979. She had been placed inside a trunk and stored in the back of a closet. By the time the body was found, it was very badly decomposed.

The authorities went to Einhorn again to question him. They told him they had found a body in his apartment. Einhorn seemed indifferent. Bail was set at $40,000 after a protracted battle by Einhorn's attorney. After further wrangling, it was agreed that Einhorn would be allowed to pay ten percent as a down payment, and the full amount would follow at a later date. The suspect convinced a wealthy friend to pay this four thousand dollars on his behalf and was allowed to walk free until the day of the trial. In 1981, just before the day of the trial, Einhorn skipped out on his bail. He fled all the way to Europe and spent the next seventeen years travelling around the continent and avoiding the authorities. He claimed residency after marrying a Swedish woman named Annika Flodin. It was decided that the trial would go on without him. In 1993, in his absence, Einhorn was found guilty to the murder of Holly Maddux and was sentenced to a life in prison, and was denied the possibility of parole. The only problem was, he was not in the country to serve his sentence.

The problem lay in America having to request Einhorn's extradition. In 1997, the authorities knew that he was living in France under an assumed name — Eugene Mallon. The process of extraditing him to face his prison sentence was incredibly complicated, far more so than anyone had originally imagined. With the diplomatic extradition treaty between the United States and France already very complicated, Einhorn spent a great deal of time trying out every single argument and avenue for potentially not having to face his punishment.

One of the main reasons for extradition to be denied is when a person is facing the possibility of the death penalty in their home country. To send them back under these conditions can be considered to passing the death sentence itself. For those countries where capital punishment is no longer practiced, this is not allowed. While Ira Einhorn was not facing the death penalty, he and his legal team argued that he might indeed be put to death should he return to the United States. Once it was established that he would not be facing the death penalty, Einhorn turned to another series of arguments. He studied French Law and approach the European Court of Human Rights. To do so required there to be another trial in cases when the defendant was not present during their own trial (known as trial *in absentia*.) Because of this, the French courts refused to permit extradition.

The failure to obtain the extradition arrangement caused a political upheaval. Thirty-five Congress members sent a communication to the then-President of France, Jacques Chirac, requesting that Einhorn be extradited.

Because of the way in which the French government is run, however, the President of France does not have the power to grant extradition in circumstances such as these. The President is prevented from issuing orders to the courts and cannot intervene in matters of extradition.

But the Pennsylvania court system was not to be defeated. A 1998 bill was put before the local governments which said that those who were originally tried *in absentia* could request another trial, which effectively removed the obstacle to Einhorn's extradition. Determined that the suspect would face the life imprisonment that had been handed out, this bill was even named 'The Einhorn Law.' Again, Einhorn and his legal team attempted to delay the possibility of returning to America. They criticized the bill as being unconstitutional and requested that the French authorities look over the changes and agree that they contravened French and European law. Again, they requested that extradition be denied.

At this point, another issue began to cause contention between the legal systems in the two countries. In the French legal system, the way in which suspects and prisoners were treated meant that Einhorn was released from custody, but under constant French surveillance.

This annoyed those in the United States who felt that it was time for Einhorn to return home and to face his punishment (or at least another trial).

It took the intervention of the French Prime Minister (France has both a President and a Prime Minister) to resolve the matter. Lionel Jospin was required to approve the extradition request. Before he could do so, more people began to offer resistance. The Green Party in France suggested that the prisoner should not be extradited, at least until the full set of issues surrounding the matter were completely settled. Jospin ignored these complaints and arranged the extradition anyway. Einhorn escalated his complaints as highly as he could, rising through the French legal system to the very top. At every level, his requests were denied.

The final means of fighting the extradition treaty occurred outside the legal system. First, facing extradition for the first time, Ira Einhorn attempted to slit his own throat. He failed in his suicide attempt. Finally, he took his case before the European Court of Human Rights. Once again, this failed. With every single attempt to avoid being sent back to America now exhausted, Ira Einhorn was sent home on the 20th of July, 2001.

Once he had returned to the United States, Einhorn faced another trial, where he was allowed to face a jury and a judge once again. This time, he was able to take to the stand and to defend himself. Once on the stand, Einhorn told a story about how Holly Maddux had actually been murdered by a group of CIA agents, who had then attempted to frame Einhorn for the murder. His own investigations into the geopolitical situation behind the Cold War and the CIA's own experiments into 'psychotronics' had led the organization to brand him as a target who needed to be eliminated. The jury took two hours to convict Einhorn for the second time. On the 17th of October, 2002, the trial that had lasted a month brought to a close the case that had lasted twenty-five years. Once again, he was sentenced to a life in prison without the possibility of parole.

While some cold cases reach a dead end because of no clues, because of bad luck, or because of human error, 'the Unicorn Killer' saw his case grow cold thanks to the difficulty of international relations.

Trying to track a man who was perpetually on the run

Victim: Cheryl Ann Commesso

Where: Pinellas County, Florida
When: 1989 (exact date unknown)
Suspect: Franklin Delano Floyd
Date of conviction: Numerous convictions

Tracking down a killer with numerous suspected attacks can be a long and difficult process. With the brutality and the aggressive nature of some of these crimes, the idea that they might be carried out by a single person can be – in some respects – comforting. The thought that there is only one person out there committing such acts is sometimes preferable to the idea that there is more than one such person. However, the concept becomes less popular when it seems that the person cannot be caught. When a case – or in this instance, several cases – go cold, the public worries that the person who could commit such heinous acts is still lurking in society. In the case of Franklin Delano Floyd and the people he attacked, this caused a great deal of fear and trouble.

Family picture of Franklin Delano Floyd and Sharon Marshall/Suzanne Maree Sevakis

The authorities' attention turned to Franklin Floyd in 1990. At this point, he was married to a woman named Sharon Marshall. When Sharon was found dead, killed in a hit-and-run accident in mysterious circumstances, Franklin was one of the prime suspects. When they looked into the woman's past, the investigators found that she had previously operated under a number of different pseudonyms. One of these was Tonya Tadlock, the name by which many of her friends and co-workers had come to know her. At the point when she died, Tadlock was also known to the authorities. Along with her husband, she was a primary suspect in the disappearance of an 18-year-old girl named Cheryl Ann Commesso. Cheryl had previously worked with

Tonya/Sharon before vanishing in 1989. Investigations into her disappearance had pointed to both Tonya and her husband Franklin as perhaps being somehow involved in the circumstances, but they were yet to be arrested. Various witness reports had suggested that the last time Commesso had been seen alive was when having a prolonged argument with Franklin Floyd. After that, she vanished.

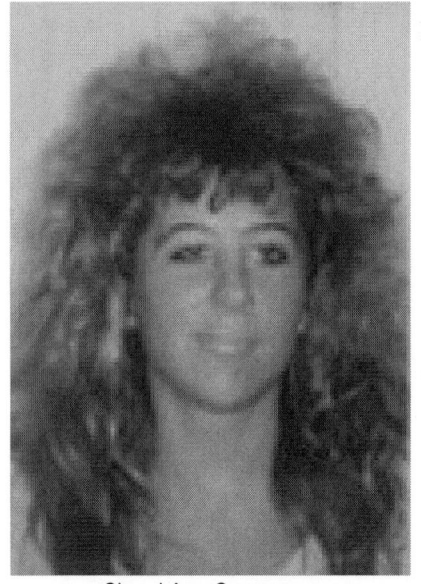

Cheryl Ann Commesso

After Sharon Marshall died, Floyd made a decision. The pair had a two-year-old son, Michael Anthony Hughes, and Floyd placed the boy into foster care before leaving the state. When quizzed about the boy, the foster parents described him to be in a terrible way. He had very limited control of his muscles, was unable to engage in verbal communication, and they reported that the child was prone to hysterical attacks and disruptive behaviour when he arrived at the foster home. Following his removal from his father, he began to make great progress, and would later begin the adoption process.

Six months later, Franklin Floyd was arrested. After he violated the terms of his parole, the courts decided that his young son would need to be investigated. To satisfy the terms of his adoption, the young boy was given a DNA test. At this time, it was discovered that Franklin Floyd was not the boy's biological father. Despite this, and following his release from jail, Franklin returned to try and take custody of the boy. Due to the fact that he had a long criminal record and was found not to be the boy's actual father, this request was not granted.

By 1984, the authorities had no new information about the disappearance of Cheryl Ann Commesso. The investigation into the hit-and-run on Sharon Marshall had not reached a satisfying conclusion. Franklin Floyd was still allowed his freedom, but was a known quantity to the authorities. Denied access to his son, he was now traveling from town to town with little to keep him rooted in any one spot.

The next incident would happen on the 12th of September, 1994. Michael Anthony Hughes was attending an elementary school and was part of the first grade. Franklin Floyd wanted his son back. He took matters into his own hands and walked into the school with a loaded gun. Accosting the principal, he demanded to be taken to his son's classroom. On arrival at the classroom, Floyd dragged both the principal and his son outside and forced them into his truck. Driving to a wooded area, they got out of the vehicle and Floyd handcuffed the principal to a tree. He then left the area in the truck, taking his son with him. The principal was found at a later date and testified against the kidnapper.

It was two months before Floyd was arrested in Kentucky. His son was nowhere to be seen — and no one has seen the boy since. Investigations into the disappearance have turned up several theories. Some have suggested that Floyd confessed that Michael died when in his care. According to other reports, Floyd claims to have drowned the young boy in a bathtub only a short time after he had taken him from the school. Similar accounts ratify this version of events, with the boy being killed by his one-time-father, with other witnesses even suggesting that they had seen the boy being buried in an unnamed cemetery.

However, some say Michal might still be alive. While Floyd has since refused to discuss the boy's current status or his possible whereabouts, he has made allusions to the boy having survived. He has frequently commented that he is 'outside the United States' or 'in Atlanta,' while refusing to go into exact details. Floyd also refuses to comment on the person who might be caring for the boy at any given moment. Some say he confessed during an interview with the FBI, but still refused to reveal any concrete information.

Investigations into Franklin Floyd's past have thrown up more and more strange circumstances. The death of Sharon Marshall and the disappearance of Cheryl Ann Commesso had both failed to reach a satisfying conclusion. With the investigations going cold, the new crimes committed by Franklin Floyd prompted the authorities to look further into the possibility that Floyd might be more involved than they had originally thought.

One of the strangest parts of the investigation into Sharon Marshall at the time found that – despite being nominally his wife – Sharon had been raised by Franklin as his daughter. From a young age, she pretended to be his child, and then later, his wife. When DNA testing was carried out on the pair, it was found that they were of no relation. After the revelation came to the forefront, Floyd refused to discuss the matter properly, having given a number of statements that contradict one another. The story of how he came to care for Sharon was confused. Sometimes he said that he rescued the little girl after her real parents had abandoned her. When searching through the records, the earliest record of Sharon was her registration for an elementary school in 1975. At this time, she had been going by the name Suzanne Davis. It is the authorities' suspicion that she had been born during the 1960s and Floyd had kidnapped her sometime between 1973 and 1975.

It was not until 2014 that the woman's true identity was revealed. Further investigations discovered that her real name had once been Suzanne Maree Sevakis. She had hailed from North Carolina and had gone missing in 1975, along with her then-stepfather, Franklin Delano Floyd. DNA testing was used to match Suzanne's mother to the samples taken after her death. At the time, Floyd had been trusted with the care of the woman's three daughters and a young son while she was forced to spend thirty days in prison for writing a bad cheque. When she was finally released, she went home to find that her husband and the children were gone. Two of the daughters were later found and returned to their mother, but Franklin, Suzanne, and the baby boy were nowhere to be seen. Nobody knows what happened to the youngest child, but Suzanne's mother attempted to file kidnapping charges against Floyd, only to be told by the local authorities that – as the children's stepfather – Floyd was well within his rights to abscond.

Sharon Marshall attended schools. She even earned a college scholarship to study aerospace engineering — but she turned it down. Rather than continuing her studying, she moved to Florida with her stepfather. In 1988, she gave birth to baby Michael. In 1989, while working as a dancer, she married Floyd and began to use the alternative name, Tonya Tadlock. This would be the name by which her co-workers and friends knew her.

But what of Cheryl Ann Commesso? Her case went cold soon after her disappearance in 1989. This lasted until 1995, when a gardener found a set of skeletal remains in Pinellas County. It would be a year before these remains were identified as Cheryl's, and investigations into the bones found that she had died after being beaten severely and being shot twice. Floyd and his wife had been named as persons of interest in the case, especially after numerous witnesses had reported a loud disagreement between Floyd and Cheryl shortly before she vanished. At the time, both Cheryl and Sharon were working as dancers in the same bar, with the argument taking place outside the establishment. Some witnesses even reported that Floyd had punched the woman. Just after Cheryl disappeared, Floyd and his wife fled the state and their trailer was burned to the ground. This disappearance made it hard to track down the people potentially involved in the case.

But another clue arrived in 1995. After purchasing a truck at an auction, a Kansas mechanic discovered that there was an envelope hidden away in the corner of the vehicle. Inside were nearly one hundred photographs, all depicting the same woman. She had been bound, gagged, and subjected to a vicious beating. The investigators were able to link the truck to Franklin Floyd. He had stolen the vehicle in 1994 and spent a month driving it around before leaving it somewhere in Texas. The clothing of the woman in the photos was compared with Cheryl's and they showed a match. The beating marks correlated with the marks on her skeleton. When looking closer, the investigators noted that many of the pieces of furniture in the images corresponded to similar items in Floyd's home. This was the evidence with which they tried Franklin Floyd with the murder of Cheryl Ann Commesso.

Despite the amount of time that has passed and the effort put into the investigation, Franklin Floyd is still only a suspect in the (supposed) death of Michael Anthony Hughes. While he has been convicted of the murder of Cheryl Commesso, the death of the young boy has still not been satisfactorily explained. When looking through the rest of the images found in the truck, investigators discovered that Floyd had also been abusing Sharon Marshall. The abuse had begun when she was very young and continued through her childhood and into adult life. It was their estimate that the sexually explicit images had been taken when Sharon was as young as four years old.

Floyd's criminal record was just as damning. Traceable back to the 1960s, when he was just a teenager, Floyd had been involved in a robbery that ended in a shootout with the local police. Further counts of abduction, rape, bank robbery, and fleeing parole all followed. At the time of Cheryl's death, Floyd was a fugitive on the run. Over time, he has been diagnosed with schizophrenia and various other conditions. Some of the authorities have requested that he be put through a mental evaluation before being tried for the murder of Cheryl Commesso, but Floyd himself rejected this idea. After a judge reversed her initial decision and found Floyd fit to stand trial, he was found guilty and sentenced to death. While the cases of the potential murders of Sharon Marshall and Michael Hughes have gone cold, Franklin Floyd has at least been found guilty of one murder. For this, he faces the death penalty.

Arresting the man fifty years after his crimes

Suspect: Gerald Mason

Where: Columbia, South Carolina
When: 1957
Date of conviction: 2003

While the majority of cold cases are remembered by the names of the victims, it can be easier to refer to others by the name of the criminal. In the case of Gerald Mason, the series of crimes he committed and the amount of time it took to track him down and bring him to justice has served to overshadow the pain and the horror of the victims in the case. With almost five decade between the initial event and the conviction, Gerald Mason's name became one of the most famous in cold case history. He was a rapist and a cop killer, and it stunned some people that it should take so long for him to be arrested and tried for his crimes.

The criminal career of Gerald Mason began from an early age. Born in 1934, he was first arrested in 1956.

After committing acts of burglary and being caught, he served time in his home state of South Carolina. Upon release, it wasn't long before he felt the need to strike again. At the age of twenty-three, he started to hitchhike across the country, stopping briefly in Louisiana to buy a gun under another name. He would later claim that this was an essential purchase to protect himself while he hitchhiked to California.

Once he reached his West Coast destination, he went to a town called Hawthorne. Here, he arrived at a local lane used by lovers for privacy. Gun in hand, he ventured down the road and found a pair of young couples at the scene. He forced all four people to strip to their underwear before tying them up and blindfolding them. Once this was done, he raped one of the young girls and left the group as they were. He stole their car and drove away, leaving the teenagers bound on the ground behind him.

While he was fleeing, Mason drove through a red light. A pair of police officers - Richard Phillips and Milton Curtis – went after him. Mason found himself in a dilemma. To hear him talk about it many years later, he felt that he was faced with a choice. Either the police officers would kill him or he would have to kill them. He waited until one of the officers turned away and drew his gun. Shooting both men, he then jumped back into the stolen car and made his getaway. When additional police units and ambulances arrived on the scene, they administered medical attention. Milton Curtis was already dead in the police car. Phillips was still alive, but was dying on the ground.

But Mason had not escaped unscathed. Phillips had managed to shoot him – though not fatally – before Mason fled the scene. Ditching the stolen vehicle and running across a number of back yards, Mason reached another road. From here, he hitchhiked away. He left little in the way of clues behind him, and there was limited technology available to detectives in the 1950s. The investigation would end up taking more than five decades.

It would take three years just to discover the weapon Mason had used during the shooting. It was found a mile away from the original crime in someone's garden. Investigators used the serial number to trace the sale of the gun to a store in Louisiana. They knew that a man calling himself George Wilson had made the purchase, but found out that this was an alias. Despite this, they managed to match the signature to one left by a man using the same name at a local YMCA. Now on the trail of this George Wilson, the investigators traced down every possible person with the name in the United States. But it came to no avail. Despite the intense search, the case went cold.

Gerald Mason went quiet. Knowing that he had committed a heinous act, he felt it best to lay low. For the next forty five years, he didn't get so much as a parking ticket. He built up a business, running a pair of service stations. He got married and started a family. By all accounts from neighbours and friends, he was a perfectly normal and even friendly man.

But technology advanced. Despite Gerald Mason laying low for almost half a century, it was 2002 when the police updated their fingerprint technology to the point where they could begin reviewing cold cases. By this time, the murder of the two policeman and the attack on the teenagers had almost been forgotten. They decided to run the prints from the stolen car through the newly developed database. They searched through results from fifty states. There was a match, deriving from a man who had been sent to prison for burglary in 1956. The man who had been imprisoned had served his time behind bars, but there was enough evidence to link him to the case. As well as the fingerprint, the handwriting samples they had from the prisoner was similar to the samples left behind by George Wilson. When linked to the murder weapon and the stolen car, the police finally had enough evidence to prompt a search for Gerald Mason.

Mason had returned to South Carolina. He had grown wealthy since the murders and was now retired. Not only did he raise a family, but he was now a grandfather. In January of 2003, a large detail of cops arrived at his home, much to his surprise. When they announced that they were from the Los Angeles Police Department, Mason realised that he would be needing a lawyer. When they told him of the crime they had arrived to investigate, Mason seemed aware of the incident.

When questioning Mason further, investigators were able to match a scar on the back of the suspect to the wound which he had obtained during the shootout with the police. It was the bullet wound inflicted by Phillips. In the face of overwhelming evidence, Gerald Mason confessed to the crimes. He claimed to have been intoxicated, that he was drunk when he came across the couples. He was still drunk when confronted by the police officers and his decision making abilities were impaired. This was the only explanation he could offer for his actions, confessing that he couldn't even remember why he had raped a girl who was then only fifteen years old.

Gerald Mason pleaded guilty to the crimes. Despite being sentenced to two life terms, he was apologetic in his conviction. He apologized to the families of the people he had hurt and mentioned that they were the crimes of a person who he was no longer able to recognize. Despite the tearful apology, one police detective felt that he was sorrier for being caught than for having committed the crimes. In 2009, Mason saw his appeal for parole turned down. It has been said by some of the prosecution team that they fully intend to ensure he serves his full life sentence. The one concession made by the judge was to allow him to serve the sentence in South Carolina, in order to be closer to his family. After five decades and after transforming himself into an entirely different person, Gerald Mason was finally forced to pay for his crimes.

The case which came to be known by a licence plate

Victim: Lil' Miss murder

Where: Billings, Montana
When: March, 1988
Suspect: Dale Eaton
Date of conviction: March, 2004

While some become known for their murderers, there have been other cold cases which have passed into local folklore under a memorable name. The 1988 disappearance of Lisa Marie Kimmell became famous under another name. Thanks to the license plate on her car, there was a catchier name for the case. Despite the troubles the investigators had in finding the perpetrator – or perhaps because of it – the 'Lil Miss' murder became one of the most famous cases in American history.

The story of the murder begins in March, 1988. On the 25th, Lisa Kimmell was working at an Arby's restaurant in Denver. She left and began the journey to the house where her parents lived, some distance away in Billings,

Montana. There was only one stop planned along the way, at a small place in Cody, Wyoming, in order to collect her boyfriend. Looking back through the records, the police in Wyoming have a report of pulling over a woman for speeding. This was just before she disappeared, and was the last confirmed sighting we have of the young woman. Despite this, there are a number of witness reports that claim to have seen a woman matching that description later in the evening. We have no way of confirming these reports, however.

It would be eight days before another trace of Kimmell was found. Her body was floating along the North Platte River when it was spotted by a local man who was fishing in the area. An autopsy found that she had been attacked — tied up, beaten, and then raped over the course of almost a week. Using other small pieces of evidence, the police could also establish that her body was transported to the Old Government Bridge. Here, her killer hit her across the head with a blunt item, gave her six stab wounds over her abdomen and chest, and then threw her into the river. Even if she had not been stabbed, the blow to the skull would have been enough to cause the death in only a short amount of time.

Interest in the case was high. Within a matter of months, the story had been featured on a number of television shows which focused on mysteries and unsolved crimes. Each time they were broadcast, there was an appeal for witnesses. The authorities described the car she had been driving when traveling to her parents' home. Thanks to the personalised licence plate that was affixed to Kimmell's car, the tag 'Lil Miss' was applied to the case. The recovery of the vehicle was, the police felt, key to the investigation. One of the most mysterious aspects of the case came from a letter than was left at her grave. Dubbing himself 'Stringfellow Hawke' (a reference to a character from the television show 'Airwolf,') the writer addressed Lisa personally. He spoke of a specific pain which never left him, and how hard he found it to get by without her. Describing her death as his own painful loss, the writer of the letter was anonymous. The investigation continued.

During this time, the highway patrol man who had pulled over Lisa for speeding became one of the suspects in the case. As the last person to see her alive, he was a key part of the investigation. However, he was acquitted of all involvement. He was able to show the authorities a taped recording of the conversation which he had with the girl when pulling her over. When the tape played in the courtroom at the eventual trial, the family members in attendance gasped and wept. Another person who was a suspect in the investigation – a person who went unnamed – was also cleared of suspicion, but committed suicide during the investigation.

During this time (in the period from 1983 to 1996), there were a series of murders throughout the area. Labelled 'the Great Basin Murders,' there was a pattern in the victims. A number of young women who were traveling through the area disappeared, only to have their bodies turn up a number of days later. Like Lisa's case, these murders occasionally became cold cases and finding the murderer proved difficult. For some people, the man who would eventually be convicted of the Lil Miss murder would emerge as one of the primary suspects in the rest of these cases.

Despite the notoriety of the murders, there were few clues as to who might have killed Lisa. The investigation ground to a halt and the Lil Miss murders became just another cold case in America. That was, until 2002. A dedicated branch of cold case investigators happened across Lisa's rape kit. They used this to develop a DNA profile of the suspect in the case. They entered this new information into the existing database and happened across a match. The man's named was Dale Wayne Eaton. At this point, he was fifty seven years old. He was also currently incarcerated. Having been convicted of a weapons charge, he was serving time in federal prison. Chasing down the story, investigators interviewed Eaton's former neighbours. When asked about the time around Lisa's disappearance, the neighbours recalled having seen the man digging a large hole in his back garden. When asked what he was doing, Eaton said that he was digging a well. While satisfied with the explanation, the neighbours remembered that it seemed strange that Eaton was only digging a hole ten feet deep. Typically, a well would need to go more than fifty feet below the surface to be functional. When examining the property, this was a spot where they investigators dug. Beneath the ground, they found Kimmell's Honda. The property was only an hour away from the last place Lisa had been seen alive. When recovering the car, investigators could instantly see the familiar 'Lil Miss' licence plate that had given the cold case its name.

Eaton was charged with the murder, as well as seven other charges related to the case. In addition to the car and the DNA, investigators traced the stereo Eaton had taken from Lisa's car and fitted into his own. They also found the alloy wheels he had taken from the car and sold to a third party. He was found guilty of the murder and the rest of the charges, and was sentenced to death.

Eaton appealed his case but was denied. He did manage to attain a stay of execution in 2009, delaying the punishment. As of the time of writing, he is currently waiting for a new sentence hearing and is still on death row.

What happens when the rich and powerful protest their innocence in a murder case?

Victim: Martha Moxley

Where: Greenwich, Connecticut
When: October, 1975
Suspect: Michael Skakel
Date of conviction: January, 2002

The murder of Martha Moxley is a cold case unlike any other. Whereas most cases gain their notoriety due to the mystery of the criminal or the brutality of the crime, the main draw for those interested in this case has been the way in which the trial has evolved. While many believe the case to have been solved, the continuing appeals and the family history of the supposed criminal have led many to question whether it has actually been solved. Whether Michael Skakel was the actual murderer, or has been unlucky enough to be convicted regardless, is not the point in question. The way in which the case has evolved demonstrates an entirely different way in which the country has dealt with this particular case.

The murder itself took place on the 30th of October, 1975. Martha went to a party with her friends. Despite being a day early, it was a Halloween party and it was to be hosted at a nearby home belonging to one of her friends, Michael Skakel. Martha and Michael's brother Thomas had been at the centre of a burgeoning romance, and friends later confessed that the two has been flirting and kissing in the time leading up to the evening in question. The last time anyone is able to recall seeing Martha, she was walking behind a fence with Thomas Skakel in the backyard of the family home, just beyond the pool.

The next day, Martha would be found beneath a tree in her own backyard. She was dead. Someone had pulled down both her trousers and her underwear, though investigators determined that she had not been the victim of a sexual assault. Close to her body, people found the remnants of a gold club that had been smashed to pieces. When conducting an autopsy, it became clear that Martha had been beaten to death using the six iron. Not only this, but she had been stabbed with the sharp shards of the smashed club. Eventually, this improvised weapon was traced to the Skakel family home.

The last person to have seen Martha alive was widely believed to have been Thomas Skakel. On the night of her death – at the party – friends had seen him with the young girl and when questioned by the police, it became clear that he only had a weak alibi. He would quickly become the prime suspect. The boy's father, an influential figure in the area, denied the police the chance to look deeper into his son's school records and mental health records. Investigations into Thomas slowed to a crawl.

Next, the police turned their attentions to Kenneth Littleton. Littleton was a tutor who has just taken up a position as a live-in educator to the Skakel family. He had only been employed for a matter of hours, being hired the day of Martha's murder. He was named as a prime suspect. Again, however, there was little evidence that could connect Kenneth to the case. Once again, the clues dried up. The investigation crawled to a halt. With no one charged, the case went cold. It spent decades in the doldrums and became one of the most famous cold cases in the area.

The notoriety of the case grew as the years passed. Primarily, this was because of the evolving alibis given by both Thomas and Michael Skakel. According to Michael's version of events, he had been creeping around outside the window of the Moxley home, peeping in through the window and masturbating while he did so. This was over an hour long period, ending at half past twelve. Two students at Michael's school, however, confessed that they had heard the boy bragging about having killed Martha using a golf club.

One of the most pressing issues was the connection that the Skakel family had to one of America's most powerful families. They were related to the Kennedys. In fact, this familial bond brought with it such privilege that a man named Greg Coleman said he once heard Michael boasting about the murder, saying that he would get away with the crime simply because of the fact that he was a Kennedy.

The case would be reopened when a fellow member of the Kennedy clan was accused of rape in 1991. William Kennedy Smith was acquitted of all charges, but not without a rumour emerging that he had been present at the party on the night Martha Moxley had died. Not only did the rumour hint that he had been present, but there was the suggestion that William might have been involved. While this rumour was quickly squashed, it did prompt investigators to reopen the case. Rushton Skakel hired his own private investigator to look into the case in 1991. This led to the assembling of a report named the Sutton Report. This was eventually leaked to the media and, inside, it contained accusations that both Thomas and Michael had altered the stories they had originally given to the police at the time. Now, their versions of events seemed to be contradictory.

It fell upon writers to bring the story greater public attention. In 1993, Dominick Dunne published a story called 'A Season in Purgatory.' The fictional narrative bore a huge amount of resemblance to the story of the murder of Martha Moxley. Another book, 'Murder in Greenwich,' went a step further and named Michael as being the person who killed Martha. Additionally, author Mark Fuhrman pointed out a number of errors in original investigation. Over the course of time leading up to the publication of the accusatory books, a number of local police officers had become convinced that the case merited further investigation.

In June of 1998, a one man grand jury began to look over the evidence in the case, a process that took eighteen months to complete. By the end, it was decided that there was enough evidence to charge Michael Skakel with the murder. Michael gave himself up that same day after a warrant for his arrest was issued and was released shortly afterwards. The bail – which was paid – was half a million dollars. Initially, it seemed the case would be tried in a juvenile court as Michael was fifteen years old at the time of the murder, but a judge eventually ruled that Michael should be tried as an adult.

The trial in question began in May of 2002. His attorney was the high-priced Michael Sherman. According to the alibi Michael gave at the time of Martha's death, he had been at his cousin's home. One of the pieces of evidence shown during the trial was the recorded conversation in which Michael Skakel discussed a book proposal. During the conversation, he discussed the night of the murder and claimed that he had been masturbating outside of a window while he sat in a tree. This could well have been the same tree where Martha's body was found the next morning. In the book proposal, it was clear that Michael was not able to confess to having carried out the murder, but nevertheless, the prosecutors took the words he was saying and laid them over images of the body as it had been found, creating an implication. During the conversation, Skakel admitted to being worried that he had been caught and then panicked.

A month after the trial began, Michael was found guilty of the murder. A judge sentenced him to serve twenty years behind bars. The use of multimedia by the prosecution and the way in which they had presented the audiotape proved to be one of the most celebrated parts of the case. But at the same time, it was also one of the most controversial. It would not be long before an appeal was launched.

Much was made of Michael Skakel's connection to the Kennedy family. Born in 1960 to Rushton Walter Skakel, he was related to Robert Kennedy. His father's sister was Robert's widow. Coupled with this, Skakel's own grandfather was a man named George, who had helped found one of the largest corporations in the history of the United States, Great Lakes Carbon. The family home was in a rich and affluent part of town. At the time of the murder, the recent death of Michael's mother had led to a growing abuse of alcohol. Not performing well at school, he eventually flunked out. His cousin, Robert F. Kennedy Junior, was one of the men who quickly came to Michael's defence. He claimed that his cousin was sensitive, that he had been the victim of an abusive father and that he had been frequently ignored as a child. This compared to neighbour's accounts of the children, saying that they were simply given as much money as they wished and left to their own devices. Michael's dependency on alcohol reached a peak in 1978 when he was arrested while driving under the influence. He was sent by the family to receive treatment. This would be the first of several stints in rehab. By the time the 1990s arrived, Michael was doing better. He not only got married and started a family, but also spent a brief career as a professional athlete, competing as a speed skater at the 1992 Olympics. Just after Michael was arrested in connection with Martha's murder, his wife filed for divorce.

After the trail finished, Michael Skakel's family came to his defence. Robert F. Kennedy Junior wrote an article for the Atlantic which caused a great deal of controversy. Labeling the trial a miscarriage of justice, he blamed an overly influential media for the conviction of his cousin. In turn, it was his suggestion that there existed additional evidence that posited Kenneth Littleton as the actual murderer. Despite the fact that the cold case had seemingly been solved, it was not allowed to stay that way.

And so began a number of appeals. Firstly came an appeal to the Connecticut Supreme Court. It failed. Then came an appeal to the Supreme Court of the United States. This also failed when they refused to hear the case. As well as swamping the legal system with a number of different methods of appeal, the family launched their own investigation into the case. Despite all of this work, in 2007 a judge refused an application for a new trial. In 2010, an appeal was again rejected. Michael Skakel and his family even turned on their original lawyer, launching a case accusing Michael Sherman of being incompetent. They suggested that Sherman had enjoyed the celebrity rather than focusing on the details of the trial.

As well as appealing against the sentence, Michael had been in jail long enough that he has been able to launch an appeal for parole. His first – in 2012 – was a failure. This was followed up with a bid to reduce the sentence which also failed. Finally, in 2013, many years of badgering the legal systems of various states resulted in Michael Skakel being granted a new trial. It was agreed that Michael Sherman was not an adequate representative. Released after paying $1.2 million in a bond, Skakel was allowed out of prison but forced to wear a GPS locator. As it stands, Michael Skakel is awaiting his new trial.

While this cold case was seemingly solved, Michael Skakel and his family (backed up by their powerful connections) have managed to throw doubt on the judgement. While it seems that this cold case had been solved, it might well be that there are more twists in the tale.

A butchered family who were killed together

Victims: McStay family

Where: Victorville, California
When: February, 2013
Suspect: Charles Merritt
Date of conviction: November, 2014

We finish our look into the history of cold cases with the disappearance of an entire family. As one of the more recent examples from the collection we have covered thus far, it proves that – even with the wealth of tools available to the investigators – it remains tough to solve every single case. When investigating a murder, one of the most important clues is the body. Without the remains, it can be incredibly hard to put together a case against any potential suspects or solve the crime itself. In the event of the McStay family murder, this was one of the major problems facing those who were looking into the family's disappearance.

Missing person poster for the McStays

Joseph and Summer McStay were a typical family. Living in Fallbrook in California, they had a four-year-old named Gianna and a three-year-old named Joseph junior. Joseph senior ran a company that specialised in building custom-made fountains, while Summer was a real estate agent. All in all, it seemed as though they were a standard American family.

This was right up until the family vanished. On the 4th of February, 2010, the last images we have of the family come from the closed circuit television of a neighbour's home. It records the family's car as it leaves the driveway in the house. This occurs at just before eight o'clock in the evening. The occupants of the car are not visible inside. Just over half an hour later, Joseph senior's cell phone placed a call to a man named Chase Merritt, who was a business associate. The call was never answered and went straight through to voicemail. According to Merritt, he was watching a film at the time and did not want to be disturbed. The call from Joseph's cell phone was traced as coming from a tower near Fallbrook.

Over the course of the next few days, numerous people tried to get in touch with the McStay family. After days of silence, Mike – Joseph's brother – jumped into the family home through an open window. The family were nowhere to be seen. In the back yard, the two dogs that belonged to the family had not been given their food. There seemed to be no signs of a struggle in the home, though there were hints the family had been in a hurry when they left. A box of eggs was left out, while two bowls of popcorn had been prepared but not eaten. The police were called.

The ensuing police investigation started by tracking the family car. It was found in the parking lot of a San Diego mall, having been towed away. It was near the Mexican border and had been towed away on the 8th of February.

It took the security guards only a few hours to determine that the vehicle had been abandoned and they had it towed. There were no clues as to where it might have been in the four days previous.

The reaction to the disappearance was huge. Those who were fascinated by unexplained mysteries immediately latched on to the case. It became the focus for large amount of analysis on the internet and even had radio shows dedicated to people going over what might have happened. A man named Rick Baker published a book on the case, wherein he explained what he learned, following events closely and had even interviewing Michael, Joseph's brother. He spent time interviewing more and more people, traveling from Belize to Mexico and the Dominican Republic to track the family down. There had been reported sightings in all of these places. Baker was particularly critical of Summer McStay and suggested that she might have killed her husband. His book was criticized by the McStay family, who doubted much of its accuracy. But the case remained a hugely interesting proposition for many people.

In November of 2013, the case changed from a disappearance to a murder investigation. Despite the case going cold, the family's remains were found in two graves outside of Victorville in California. They were discovered by a motorcyclist who was passing through the area. It took a couple of days for the bodies to be identified as belonging to the McStay family, but they were soon ruled to be the victims of a quadruple homicide. According to police reports, it seemed as though the family had all died after receiving strong blows to the head using a blunt object. There were indications that it might have occurred when the family were still at home. When discussing the case, the authorities refused to delve into possible motives or causes for the family's murder. This was followed up by accusations and formal complaints from the extant McStay family about the way in which the case was handled.

After the discovery of the bodies, Rick Baker offered refunds to people who had purchased his book. There were suggestions that Mexican drug cartels might have been behind the murders, but Baker was dismissive of such suggestions. While some had earlier suggested that the McStay family might have left of their own volition, it was now clear that this was unlikely to be the case. The family's bank accounts – which held close to one hundred thousand dollars – also had not been touched. Despite this large amount of capital, there were growing suggestions that the McStays had not been entirely secure in their finances. A neighbour suggested that they might have been on the verge of eviction before they had purchased their home in Fallbrook. These suggestions were also denied at a later date.

Deepening the mystery was the fact that Summer McStay had used a variety of names during her life time. She had been born as Virginia Lisa Aranda, but had at various points been known by Summer Martelli, Lisa Aranda-Martelli, Lisa Aranda, Lisa Martelli and Summer Aranda-Martelli. She also lied about her age, though this was usually just in public rather than on official documents. While some thought this part of the mystery, family members filed away these irregularities as just her minor idiosyncrasies.

One of the chief suspects in the case was Chase Merritt. With numerous felony convictions, he was asked to take a polygraph test by the police. He passed. Eventually, in November of 2014, Chase Merritt was arrested in connection with the murder. As a business partner of Joseph McStay, he had spent a large amount of time with the man in the run up to the family's disappearance. His DNA was found in the family's car. With a growing case of evidence, the sentence has not yet been handed out. Despite this, the district attorney remains confident enough in reaching a guilty verdict that he is pursing the death penalty. As of the time this book was written, Chase Merritt is awaiting trial. After it begins on August the 10th, 2015, we may know for sure whether this cold case can truly be closed for the final time.

Conclusion

Solving a cold case is one of the hardest prospects known to our police forces. As the time from the crime increases, witnesses' memories become fuzzy, evidence is lost, clues are buried and all manner of ill fortune can befall an investigation. Perhaps this is why it is so satisfying when cases such as those detailed in this book are finally brought to a conclusion. As well as seeing justice finally served, we are given the chance to witness what is often years of work being poured into one case and can see the satisfactory conclusion of an enduring mystery.

As the technology employed by police forces gets better and better, we might find ourselves with an increasing ability to look over the old cases on our books and be able to put many of them to bed. Much in the way that DNA evidence is able to solve some mysteries there and then, and even go back over older mysteries and lay them to rest, who is to say what technologies we might have in the future? One day, the prospect of a case going this long without being solved might well be a thing of the past.

But one of the most important elements in all of these investigations is hard work. Often, a cold case is solved simply because someone refused to give up the possibility that the answers are out there. From family members, to friends, to police officers, and simply interested third parties, those who work hard to solve the cold cases often have our everlasting thanks. Not only do they often make for great stories, but they help tie up the loose ends that can be so thoroughly unsatisfactory.

If you have an interest in learning more about cold cases, as well as the techniques that are used to solve them, then read on and find a Further Reading section at the end of this book. For those of us who are simply fascinated by the numerous cold cases that still exist in the world, maybe one day these too will be solved.

Further Reading

Aron, P. (1998). Unsolved Mysteries of American History. New York: Wiley.

Branson, J. and Branson, M. (2011). Delayed Justice. Amherst, N.Y.: Prometheus Books.

Douglas, J. and Olshaker, M. (2001). The Cases that Haunt Us. New York: Pocket Books.

Halber, D. (n.d.). The Skeleton Crew.

Newton, M. (2009). The Encyclopedia of Unsolved Crimes. New York: Facts on File.

Odell, R. (2010). The Mammoth Book of Bizarre Crimes. Philadelphia, Pa.: Running Press Book Pub.

Philbin, T. (2012). The Killer Book of Cold Cases. Naperville, Ill.: Sourcebooks.

Ramsland, K. (2004). The Science of Cold Case Files. New York: Berkley Boulevard Books.

Photography Credits

Theodore Kaczybsku

"Theodore Kaczynski" by Federal Bureau of Investigation - Uploaded from http://www.thesmokinggun.com/mugshots/celebrity/killers/ted-kaczynski; original source is the Federal Bureau of Investigation. Licensed under Public Domain via Commons.

Centennial Park Bombing

"Olympic Park Panorama" by veggiefrog - Flickr: Olympic Park Panorama. Licensed under CC BY 2.0 via Commons

Barbara Ann Taylor

"Barbara Ann Hackmann Taylor" by Source. Licensed under Fair use via Wikipedia.

Scott Erskrine

"Scott T. Erskine". Via Wikipedia

Ira Einhorn

"Ira Einhorn" by Original uploader was Salomon at fr.wikipedia - Transferred from fr.wikipedia. Licensed under Public Domain via Commons -

Chreyl Ann Commesso

"Cheryl Ann Commesso" by Source (WP:NFCC#4). Licensed under Fair use via Wikipedia -

Franklin Delano Floyd

"Franklin Delano Floyd and Sharon Marshall" by Source (WP:NFCC#4). Licensed under Fair use via Wikipedia -

Martha Moxley

"MarthaMoxley" by Source. Licensed under Fair use via Wikipedia -

The McStay Family

"McStay family" by Source (WP:NFCC#4). Licensed under Fair use via Wikipedia -

More Books from Andrew J. Clark

Just click on the book covers to check them out

Solving Cold Cases: True Crime Stories that Took Years to Crack

These true murders baffled the authorities for years before being solved.

Bone chilling murder and disappearance cases that took years to crack. Now, thanks to new technologies, advanced in forensic science and profiling techniques, these cases were solved and families could finally know what happened. The cases in this new book from Clark come from the USA, United Kingdom and Canada. You will read about ingenious methods that some investigators had to resort to in order to solve cases that were thought to be more and more unsolvable as time passed.

Vanished: Chilling True Stories of Missing Persons Missing People Case Files

Chilling true stories of People Gone Missing

Of the millions who go missing every year around the world, there are those who simply vanish and are never seen again. The sheer volume of people who disappear each and every year are, when examined in detail, terrifying. In this book, we will touch upon some of the most terrifying, touching, strange, and worrying stories

Missing Person Case Files Solved: People Gone Missing and Found Again True Stories of Mysterious Disappearances

Lost and Found...True stories of person who vanished in thin air and were found months and even years, decades later.

Read about their mysterious and sometime bone chilling stories like the boy whose kidnap inspired a search and rescue team or the actress who vanished without a warning and much more.

Kidnapped...True and Chilling Stories of People Who Were Taken Against Their Will

Abducted...True stories that will leave you speechless. Read the horrific and disturbing true kidnapping case files.

Kidnappings are far more common than we might imagine. Rather than simply being something that we see in film and television, every year there are real people who are abducted, taken from their homes, and not allowed to return. Sometimes the motivations are financial, sometimes they are sexual. Every time, they are criminal acts involved. In this book, we will be looking through some of the strangest, most violent, and most notorious cases of kidnapping.

Printed in Poland
by Amazon Fulfillment
Poland Sp. z o.o., Wrocław